DECODA

⦗Harcourt

⦙o   Boston   Dallas   Chicago   San Diego

Visit The Learning Site!

www.harcourtschool.com

ISBN 0-15-326684-8

12 13 179   10 09 08 07 06

Ordering Options
ISBN 0-15-323767-8 (Collection)
ISBN 0-15-326718-6 (package of 5)

Contents

The Sack

by
J.C. Cunningham

illustrated by
Gary Taxali

Nick has a sack.

What did Nick pack
in his sack?

Is it a cat?
Is it a hat?

What did Nick pack
in his sack?

Can I kick it?
Can I pick it?

What did Nick pack
in his sack?

7

Look what's in
the sack! Mmmm!

Pack the
Van

by Rose Fabian
illustrated by Dennis Hockerman

Rick! Pack the
mitts in a sack.

Nick can help.

Mack! Pack the
bats in a sack.

Nick can help.

Mick! Pick up a sack.
Nick can help.

Jack! Back up.
Come back, back,
back.

Nick can help!

The Sack

Word Count: 49

High-Frequency Words

look
the
what
what's

Decodable Words*

a
can
cat
did
has
hat
his
I
in
is
it
kick
mmmm
Nick
pack
pick
sack

*Words with /k/*ck* appear in **boldface** type.

Pack the Van

Word Count: 41

High-Frequency Words

come
help
the
up

Decodable Words*

a
back
bats
can
in
Jack
Mack
Mick
mitts
Nick
pack
pick
Rick
sack
van

*Words with /k/*ck* appear in **boldface** type.